It's All About Order

by J. K. Schmauss
illustrated by Maurie Manning

HOUGHTON MIFFLIN   BOSTON

Printed in China

ISBN 10: 0-618-89983-9
ISBN 13: 978-0-618-89983-8

11 12 13 14 15 16 0940 21 20 19 18 17 16
4500607571

Who's Tallest?

There are seven children in my class,
And that includes me, too.
Harry is the tallest one.
The shortest one is Drew.

Maria comes after Harry,
And Marco comes before Drew.
Kim is in the middle,
And that leaves only two.

Leon started out real small,
But then he grew and grew.
He's taller now than Kim is—
He'll catch up to Harry, too.

I'm taller now than Marco,
And I do believe it's true—
Though I'm not as tall as Kim is,
I might be before I'm through!

Tall to short, short to tall,
An order, it is true,
Arranges things by trait
Such as height or value.

Read·Think·Write What order should the children be in from tallest to shortest?

Roberto's Warehouse

Roberto opened a warehouse.
It was full of nails and screws.
He sold his wares
In trios and pairs
To builders and others to use.
He'd invested a lot of dollars—

Twenty-three thousand, eight hundred forty-four.
It had taken two years
of work, sweat, and tears,
But he expected to earn much more.

Roberto was always busy
But decided it had to be known.
Just what was the count?
What was the amount?
What would tell him his business had grown?

So Roberto began his accounting.
It gave him the answer he sought.
Fifty-four thousand ten,
He wrote with his pen.
"Not a bad profit," he thought.

For if you compare
Twenty-three thousand, eight hundred forty-four
With fifty-four thousand ten,
On a number line or with place value then
You can clearly see which is more.

Read·Think·Write How did Roberto know he had
made a profit?

Rounding

"Let's say you have a number—
The number is 632.
How do you round it to the nearest 100?"
the teacher asks of Lou.

Lou thinks of what the teacher said
So many times this week.
He gathers up his courage
And he begins to speak.

"When a digit is less than 5,
down the number goes.
But if a digit is 5 or more,
then the number grows.

"I start with the digit on the right.
I see that it's a 2.
It's less than 5, so I round it down
To a 0—That's what I do.

"In the tens place there's a 3,
Which is also less than 5.
I change the 3 to 0;
600 is where I arrive."

hundreds   tens   ones

6   3   2

So practice doing rounding
With any numbers that you see.
Start at the right and move to the left
It's as simple as can be!

Read·Think·Write What would 5,642 be rounded to the nearest hundred?

1. What are two ways to compare numbers?
2. What do you call arranging a group of objects by a certain trait or characteristic?
3. Round 355 to the nearest ten.
4. If you knew the ticket prices for every ride you wanted to go on at an amusement park, what would you do to figure out about how much money you should bring?

    A. Compare the ticket prices and then add.
    B. Order the ticket prices and then add.
    C. Round the ticket prices and then add.

Activity

Understand Genres Write a poem of 8 lines or more about numbers. You can write about comparing numbers, ordering numbers, or rounding numbers. Share your poem with a partner. Have partners check to make sure the math vocabulary was used correctly.